1 Conservation and developmen[t]

People use the Earth's **resources** to try and improve their lives – that is **development.** They need to look after the Earth to make sure it continues to provide the resources – that is **conservation.** Finding the right balance between development and conservation is one of the major tasks facing people today.

The growth of **industrialised** societies has brought huge changes to the lives of people living in them, mainly for the better. People are healthier and live longer, largely because there are secure supplies of good food, good medical care, better housing and working conditions and improved education. The standard of living has improved with people now enjoying all manner of consumer goods from radios to motor cars. All these changes have contributed to improvements to our quality of life.

The improvements ha[ve] progress in science an[d] finds out about the forces of nature and technology attempts to harness these forces. Agriculture and industry have applied this knowledge to their activities. However, in doing this the **environment** is changed and sometimes damaged. We need to know more about how the world works and what effects our activities are likely to have on the natural processes that supply our food, air, water and countless other resources we depend on. It is a task that governments, industry, environmental groups, teachers and individuals can work on together. It is necessary if we are to have a world that is productive and pleasant to live in.

> 'We are now just beginning to realise that we must find an alternative to our misplaced belief that there is a choice between economy and the environment.'
>
> **From 'Our Common Future', the 1987 report of the Brundtland Commission on Environment and Development.**

2 Sources of energy

Using energy enables us to enjoy a high standard of living. This chapter shows that obtaining these fuels can damage the environment and explains how the industries involved are trying to protect the environment.

Three quarters of the world's population live in developing countries. They consume barely a quarter of the world's energy.

The need to use energy

The industrialised society is dependent upon using energy from fossil fuels such as coal and oil. It is appropriate therefore, to start this book by showing how we obtain such fuels.

Oil, coal and gas are fossil fuels that once used are gone forever. They are called non-renewable sources of energy. It is also possible to obtain energy from atoms (nuclear power) and other sources that can last forever (renewable) such as winds, waves, tides, and wood.

Coal, oil and natural gas not only provide fuel for vehicles, power stations and machines in industry; they are also raw materials from which many products are made including fertilisers, plastics, artificial fibres, lubricants, medicines and a whole range of chemicals. When we consider how obtaining these products can damage the environment, we must also consider the benefits that we enjoy from using them. Any discussion about fossil fuels is not on whether we should use them or not — but how we should control the use of them to protect the quality and health of the environment, and conserve a valuable non-renewable resource.

Every year, on average, each person in Britain consumes as much energy as there is in five tonnes of coal. The situation is very different in **Third World** countries. Almost 75 per cent of the world's population live in these countries, yet they only use 15 per cent of these non-renewable resources. Instead they rely on wood, animal dung and animal power for the small amounts of energy they use in farming, heating and cooking. An average North American consumes 330 times more energy than a person living in Ethiopia.

Fossil fuels and the environment

Fossil fuels represent a huge store of energy from the Sun that was used by plants and animals millions of years ago. By using coal, oil and gas, the industrialised countries are able to use the energy that nature put 'in the bank' millions of years ago. However, fossil fuels will run out, possibly within the next 100 years.

Oil and natural gas

Britain takes most of its oil and gas from underneath the sea bed using production platforms situated out at sea where conditions

For the majority of people in the world, wood is the most important fuel (left). Developed countries, such as Britain, rely on fossil fuels (right).

Technology in the North Sea. Oil rigs like these produce millions of gallons of oil which we depend upon in our everyday life.

can be very rough. Technology has been pushed to the limits to extract these valuable resources, but the price has on occasions been high. In 1988, an explosion destroyed the oil rig Piper Alpha and killed 167 people (see Industry and the environment).

Oil spills can occur when the oil is being transported from the place of production to the refineries. In March 1989 the tanker Exxon Valdez set off from the port of Valdez in Alaska with a cargo of crude oil. Minutes later it ran aground and 44 million litres of oil poured into the sea over several days. The huge quantity of oil released means that it is impossible to clear up all of it. Wildlife, especially birds and sea mammals such as sea otters and seals, has been devastated and many fishermen are being compensated for the loss of their livelihoods. In the cold climate of Alaska the oil will only break down slowly. It will probably take ten years for the environment to return to near normal.

The company has accepted the principle that 'the polluter pays' as well as responsibility for the clean up. It is costing about $800 million. However, many local people are still not satisfied that enough is being done.

In Britain only small quantities of oil and natural gas are extracted on land. There is, however, an extensive network of pipelines

Clearing up oil spills at sea

Accidents are rare, but when oil spills occur the oil industry has emergency procedures to minimise any damage.

1 *Dispersants:* Strong detergents can be sprayed on to the oil. These cause it to break up more quickly. However, dispersants cannot be used close to the shore or near fisheries as the chemicals are poisonous to marine life.

2 *Sinking:* Oil floats on the surface, but powdered chalk spread on the surface absorbs the oil and makes it sink. Although the surface is cleared quickly, the oil ends up on the sea bed where it can continue to damage the plants and animals living there.

3 *Absorption:* Materials such as straw, peat and polystyrene can be put on the water to absorb the oil. They continue to float and can be collected and disposed of. This method can only be used in calm conditions.

4 *Booms:* Floating barriers can be placed in the water to prevent the oil from spreading on to nearby beaches and wildlife areas. Small slicks can be surrounded by booms and the oil sucked from the surface into a tanker. Calm water is needed.

5 *Leave it:* If the oil spill is far out to sea, it is often best to leave it and let natural processes break it up.

under the ground and many refineries and storage depots have been built at ground level. Before any building takes place, landscape and ecological studies are undertaken to ensure that any damage is kept to a minimum.

Drilling for oil at Wytch Farm, Dorset. BP has gone to great lengths to minimise damage to the environment.

A spectacular site of an open cast mine in South Wales.

Coal mining

Open cast mining: British Coal aims to produce about 15 million tonnes of coal a year from open pits. In open cast mining, the surface soil and rocks are removed by a huge dragline to reach the coal seams below. This sometimes creates holes up to 200 metres deep. The largest site covered 800 hectares at Butterwell in Northumberland. It is now true that all such sites are filled in when mining work has been completed, so that the land can be used again.

Before British Coal can excavate a site, it has to receive planning permission from the local council. The Department of the Environment states that applications should only be turned down if 'there are overriding environmental considerations'. Environmental groups fear that this directive is not strong enough to protect the environment. A new site approved for mining at Lomax near Manchester contains 12 ponds. These are among the most important sites in the country for the rare great crested newt. There are plans to remove the newts in an attempt to re-establish them in neighbouring ponds, but no one knows if this will be successful or not.

Deep mining: Most of Britain's coal is mined from seams deep underground and is reached by shafts dug from the surface. British Coal is opening new 'super-pits' to exploit richer coal seams which can be mined at a lower cost.

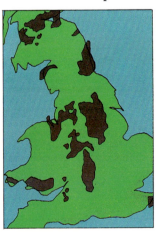

Coal mining regions in Britain.

Modern pit head buildings in Yorkshire's Kellingley Colliery.

CASE STUDY

Opening a new coalmine in the Midlands

Model of the planned new Hawkhurst Moor mine near Coventry.

British Coal is planning to open a new mine at Hawkhurst Moor on the western outskirts of Coventry. The mine is opposed by many local people and a public enquiry has been held.

Economic arguments

During the 10-year construction period, 700 jobs will be created. When the mine is working it will create 1800 new jobs. Fifty per cent of the £400 million investment will be spent with local firms. High quality coal will be available to industry at competitive prices.

It is impossible to predict what the market for coal will be when production starts in 1999. It could be cheaper to import coal.

Environmental arguments

Forty hectares of the site will be landscaped to protect the local people from noise and dust and to hide the buildings.

The mine will occupy 105 hectares of countryside in the narrow green belt that separates Coventry from Birmingham. The landscape will be spoilt and the area will become noisy and dirty. It will not be possible to enjoy the countryside any more.

There will be no lorry movements at night. To keep lorries off small roads, a new link to the main road will be built. Sixty per cent of the coal will be taken away by rail.

Mining will result in 1000 lorry movements a day in an area that is already busy. It will create dust, noise and congestion.

The coal waste will be used to fill unused quarries nearby, reclaiming more land than is taken by the mine. Reclamation can be planned to make new areas for recreation and conservation.

600 000 tonnes of waste will be transported away from the site to old quarries which would be better left as conservation sites.

Finding the balance

Fossil fuels are essential for maintaining our ways of life, but obtaining them will always change the environment. There is now much more control of mining operations. The **European Community** requires that a study of the impact on the environment of all major projects is carried out. The results of these studies can be used to make sure that the project damages the environment as little as possible. This may add to the costs and put up the price of energy. Balancing the interests of the energy industry, the economy, people and the environment is not easy. It is eventually up to us to decide what is an acceptable balance between protecting the environment and protecting our life styles.

WHAT YOU CAN DO

1 We can reduce the amount of fossil fuels used by not wasting energy. Working in a small group, write down ways in which you think you could save energy. Then draw up a statement of what *you* are going to do and attempt to stick to it.

2 Using a diagram of your school, mark and make notes on how energy could be saved.

PAUSE FOR THOUGHT

You live in a small town situated in the green belt between two large conurbations, like Hawkhurst Moor. It is proposed to open a coal mine within sight of your home. Consider how you think you would react to this proposal if you:

a) Worked in an office in the nearby city.
b) Were a woman and out of work.
c) Were a man and out of work.
d) Owned a small haulage business.
e) Worked for British Coal.

in Britain

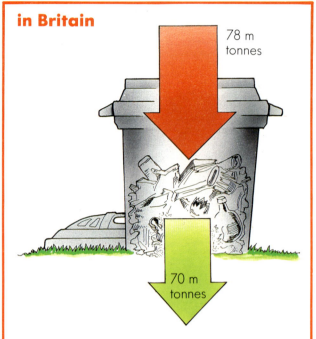

Of the 78 million tonnes of glass, paper, food etc that is dumped into the dustbin every year, about 70 million tonnes ends up in the ground. Most of it could be recycled or used as fuel. It could save Britain the equivalent of 12–14 million tonnes of coal a year.

Every year each person throws away

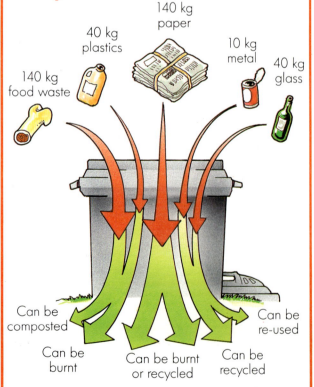

Most of our rubbish can be either burnt or recycled. If burnt the incinerator must be carefully controlled to as not to pollute the air.

3 Using energy

Fumes from burning fossil fuels can pollute the atmosphere. This section looks at the damage that is being caused and some of the solutions.

The environmental consequences of burning fossil fuels

Vile smelling, smoke-laden smogs were common in winter in most industrial towns until the 1950s. They were caused by burning coal which produced soot, smoke and fumes. Often it was not possible to see more than a few metres, but more seriously, smog killed people, especially those with breathing problems. During a very bad smog in London from 5–9 December 1952, the number of deaths per day increased from 250 to 1000.

The Clean Air Act of 1956 led to the creation of smokeless zones in which non-smokey fuels such as coke, gas, oil and electricity had to be used. The air is now much cleaner and smogs are a feature of the past, but the invisible fumes from fossil fuels are still causing problems.

Acid deposition (acid rain)

Acid rain damages lakes, rivers, trees and forests in many parts of the world, especially in Canada, USA, Scandinavia, Britain and the mainland of Europe. When fossil fuels are burnt, sulphur in the fuel is turned into the gas sulphur dioxide. Gaseous oxides of nitrogen are formed as well. If these are released into the atmosphere, some may settle on surrounding vegetation as dry deposition. The remainder is carried away in the air where the oxides and water vapour can react in the presence of **ultraviolet** light to produce dilute sulphuric (H_2SO_4) and nitric (HNO_3) acids. Eventually, these acids reach the ground as rain, snow or mist. Some rain is so polluted that it is one thousand times more acid than normal rain. The **pollution** in the air can be carried for hundreds of kilometres by the wind before it is precipitated, and can cause damage a long way from the source of pollution. Norway, for example, receives 200 000 tonnes of sulphur dioxide from other countries every year.

Acid rain is most damaging where the environment cannot neutralise the **acids.** Chalky soils such as those on the Downs of southern England, are **alkaline** and neutralise the acid. They have a high **buffering capacity.** In areas of hard acidic rocks, such as granite, the soil has a low buffering capacity and land and water become more acid. Large areas of

The damaging effects of acid rain on conifer trees in Sweden (above), and on the stone carvings on Stirling Castle, Scotland (below).

Canada and Scandinavia are granite and it is here that the problems are most severe.

As lakes become acid, the wild plants and animals in them suffer. When the **pH** falls from a healthy 6.5 to an unhealthy 4.5 (ie 100 times more acid) most life in the lake is lost. Trees too are affected, especially conifers. In Czechoslovakia, several forests in the hills have been completely destroyed and the landscape is treeless.

The damage is not restricted to trees and lakes. Stonework on buildings is dissolved and agricultural production may be reduced. Water from wells is sometimes unfit to drink because aluminium and other heavy metals in the ground are more soluble in acid water and are carried through the soil into water supplies.

Global warming/The greenhouse effect

When fossil fuels are burnt, carbon dioxide is formed. About 20 000 million tonnes of carbon dioxide are put into the atmosphere every year from human activities. The gas forms a very small proportion of the atmosphere. However, over the last 100 years or so, the amount of carbon dioxide in the air has increased from 265 parts per million to 350 parts per million, an increase of around 30 per cent.

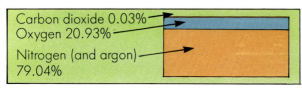

Gaseous composition of the atmosphere.

Carbon dioxide is one of about 30 'greenhouse' gases which help to maintain the temperature of the earth. Without them, the Earth would be 40 degrees Celsius cooler and too cold for any life as we know it. As the amount of these gases increases, the Earth becomes warmer. Scientists consider that the build up of carbon dioxide and other greenhouse gases in the atmosphere will cause the average temperature on the surface of the Earth to increase by at least one to one-and-a-half degrees Celsius by the middle of the next century.

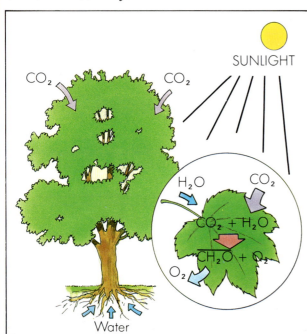

The energy from the Sun is used by all living plants in a process called photosynthesis. The sunlight is trapped by the green chlorophyll and used in the manufacture of carbohydrate from carbon dioxide, and water drawn in from the soil by the roots. Oxygen is a by-product of this reaction.

1 Incoming visible light from the Sun (long-wave radiation) passes through the atmosphere and heats the Earth's surface.

2 Some heat radiation (short-wave) escapes back to space, but the rest is trapped by greenhouse gases.

3 A build-up of gasses, including carbon dioxide, CFCs, methane and nitrogen oxides prevent heat radiation escaping to space. This results in global warming.

The greenhouse effect.

As a result of this temperature rise, sea levels will probably rise by a metre or more by the year 2050 due to the melting of the polar ice-caps and expansion of the sea water. Wealthy nations might be able to afford to build extra sea defences to protect the land, but poorer nations are probably doomed to suffer more frequent catastrophic floods. About 20 per cent of Bangladesh is likely to be inundated, forcing millions of people from their homes.

The Earth's climatic belts might shift and some of the world's major food producing areas, such as the prairies of the USA, might then become too dry for arable farming. Climatic figures collected for hundreds of years will no longer provide a reliable guide for planners of dams, irrigation and drainage schemes as well as of others that must be designed to remain safe in extreme conditions of weather.

Scientists cannot predict accurately how the greenhouse effect will change the world. Why do you think this is?

A power station for electricity generation.

Finding the balance

Saving energy: A lot of the energy in fossil fuels is wasted when it is burnt. A coal-fired power station only turns 30 per cent of the energy in the coal into electricity. The rest usually ends up warming the atmosphere. Denmark uses this energy to heat homes and factories in the vicinity instead. The developed countries of the world could use less fuel without suffering a drop in their standard of living if they spent more money on energy conservation. Individually, we can all help by turning out lights when they are not needed, turning down the heating a little and wearing an extra sweater, walking or cycling instead of asking for a lift in the car, closing doors and so on.

Controlling pollution

Nature is capable of processing a certain amount of pollution and making it safe, but not on the scale that is now needed to clean up the atmosphere. Scandinavian countries, for example, estimate that sulphur dioxide production must be cut by 80 per cent if their environment is to recover.

Pollution control: Most types of air pollution caused by fossil fuels can be eliminated. The Central Electricity Generating Board is now fitting desulphurisation equipment which will take out 90 per cent of the sulphur from the fumes emitted from some of its largest coal-fired power stations. Over the next 10 years, £1.5 billion will be spent. It will add 10 per cent to the cost of electricity.

A desulphurisation unit uses between 200 000 and 330 000 tonnes of limestone a year. But could the solution of one environmental problem lead to others? Limestone comes from quarries. Many people may oppose the expansion of existing quarries or the opening of new ones.

Using less polluting fuels: Some fossil fuels are 'cleaner' than others. Most natural gas contains very little sulphur. It also produces fewer oxides of nitrogen and only 50 per cent of the carbon dioxide of coal for the same amount of energy. There are also less conventional fuels, such as ones derived from animal or vegetable waste. When materials decompose, methane is produced and this can be used in a similar way to natural gas. This form of alternative energy is already being used successfully.

Biotechnology: Bacteria developed in the laboratory may be able to carry out many of the processes that now require a lot of energy. For example, by using bacteria, copper can be produced from rock without smelting. Bacteria can also make some dangerous chemicals safe without the need for burning at high temperatures. But there may be new environmental problems if human-made organisms are released into the environment and then behave in unexpected ways.

Alternative sources of energy

Although harmful gases like sulphur dioxide and oxides of nitrogen can be prevented from getting into the air, carbon dioxide still remains a problem. The only effective way of reducing carbon dioxide emissions is to use less fossil fuel. Energy conservation will help, but the demand for energy will continue to increase, especially if we are sincere in our efforts to improve the living conditions of those living in developing countries. Other 'clean' sources of energy are needed. The use of lead-free petrol and catalytic converters is becoming increasingly common.

The nuclear option

Since the 1950s, a lot of money has been spent on developing nuclear power. It is now responsible for providing two per cent of the world's energy and 15 per cent of all the electricity generated. One advantage of nuclear power is that it does not create the pollution problems associated with burning fossil fuels.

However, like all human activities, it has costs as well as benefits. The current intense debate is about whether the environmental costs and risks are worth the benefits.

Pollution

FOR: Nuclear power stations add very little radiation to the environment. Eighty-seven per cent of all the radiaton we receive is from natural sources. Of the rest, most comes from medical sources including X-rays and radiation therapy to cure cancer.

AGAINST: Nuclear power stations increase **radiation** in the environment. High levels of radiation are known to lead to an increased risk of cancer.

The Torness advanced gas-cooled nuclear reactor may not cause the same pollution effects that fossil fuels do, but there are other possible implications for the environment.

Safety

FOR: Reactors are designed to very high safety standards. Even if there is an accident, modern power stations have protective containment buildings which will prevent any escape of radioactive materials. Nuclear power stations have a better safety record than almost all other human activities and the risk to the public from British nuclear power stations is negligible.

AGAINST: There have been accidents at Sellafield (Britain), Three Mile Island (USA) and Chernobyl (USSR). The possibility of a further disastrous accident like that at Chernobyl is a risk that has to be avoided at all costs.

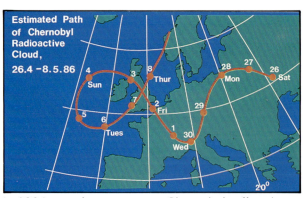

In 1986 a nuclear reactor at Chernobyl suffered a serious accident killing 31 people, sending a cloud of radioactive gases and dust into the atmosphere which affected much of Europe. Radiation in the area is still so high that nobody will be allowed to live permanently within 30 kilometres of the plant for at least 50 years. (Copyright remains the property of the National Radiological Protection Board).

Disposal of waste

There is already waste from power stations and other nuclear sources that has to be disposed of. The amount of waste from nuclear installations is very small in comparison with other forms of power production. It has been decided to deposit low and intermediate level waste in a deep underground site where there is virtually no risk of radioactivity ever reaching people.

Nuclear power generates radioactive waste. Some has to be kept safely for thousands of years. It is not right to expect future generations to look after our waste, and no method of disposal can guarantee to be 100 per cent safe.

Wherever radioactive materials are used radioactive waste is generated. This has to be disposed of safely so that any radiation cannot damage people or other living things. Waste is divided into three categories:

Low level waste This is only slightly radioactive and includes such waste as discarded protective clothing.
Intermediate level waste This can be up to 1000 times more radioactive. It includes the containers in which nuclear fuel is held. It is set in concrete and steel before disposal.
High level waste is up to 1000 times more radioactive than intermediate level waste and includes the old fuel rods from power stations. There is very little of it and it can continue to be kept at the surface and its safety carefully monitored.

Low and intermediate level waste will be disposed of in specially built underground caverns at least 300 metres deep where radioactivity is most unlikely to reach the human environment (see diagram). Only one site is needed and it will receive the equivalent of 15 train loads of waste a week.

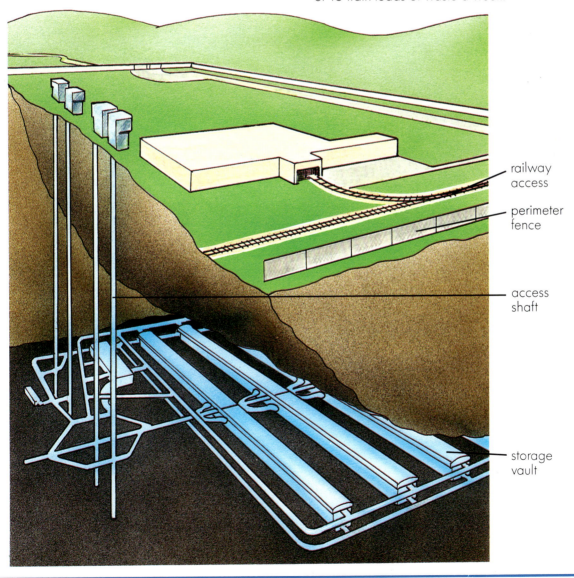

- railway access
- perimeter fence
- access shaft
- storage vault

Other sources of energy

Energy from the sun and in the wind, rivers, oceans and rocks can all be harnessed. These are renewable sources of energy but like all human activities, they too have an impact on the environment. They are unlikely to be able to provide the current energy needs of the world.

Wind power — huge windmills use the energy in the wind to generate electricity.

Wind is free and non-polluting. Tests show that windmills can produce electricity economically in some areas.

Large areas of ground are needed in exposed areas (often of great beauty), to build enough windmills to harness the energy in useful quantities. They are noisy, unsightly, and can interfere with TV reception. They do not work when there is no wind.

Wind generator at Carmarthen Bay, Wales.

Tidal barrages — dams built across tidal river estuaries use the flow of the tides to drive turbines to generate electricity.

The tides are free and the energy produced does not pollute the atmosphere. Although building costs are high, running costs can be low.

Barrages can upset the ecology of an estuary. For this reason they are usually opposed by nature conservation groups. Estuaries will be more prone to suffer pollution from other sources as they will not be so easily flushed out by the river.

Tidal barrage scheme on the estuary of the River Rance in northern France.

Hydroelectric power — uses water released from human-made lakes to drive turbines to generate electricity. They are built on major rivers, eg the Aswan Dam on the Nile, or in mountainous areas.

This is a well proven technique which already provides 25 per cent of the world's electricity at low cost. There is no pollution of the atmosphere. Lakes can improve the ecology of an area and create opportunities for fishing and recreation.

Artificial lakes flood large areas of land — often the best agricultural land in the area. Flooding damages the native ecology and disrupts the lives of local people. Many of the best sites for such schemes have already been developed. Dams sometimes break and the rush of water can kill people and ruin the land.

Sloy Dam, Loch Lomond, one of many hydroelectric schemes in Scotland.

Outlook

Providing people with the energy they need without damaging or destroying the environment is one of the urgent problems to be resolved. Burning fossil fuels has to be phased out because, as well as polluting the atmosphere, they will eventually run out. We should also consider if oil, coal and gas which provide us with many important industrial products (from plastics to medicines), should just be burnt.

There are alternatives, but they all have their advantages and disadvantages. What should our policy be?

Moving goods and people through the environment

During this century there has been a huge growth in the movement of goods and people around Britain, particularly since the 1950s. Road transport has been the major focus for this growth. Lorries carry 80 per cent of all goods, and 82 per cent of all the kilometres travelled by people take place in a car.

Britain has one of the highest densities of road traffic in the world. If current trends continue, traffic on the roads will increase by more than 30 per cent during the next 10 years. There is already severe traffic congestion in many towns and on many trunk roads and motorways at peak periods. If more land is not taken for building roads, the cost of traffic congestion will escalate. Congestion already costs over £3.2 billion a year in lost time and wasted fuel.

When individuals and industry choose which form of transport to use, their decision is most often based on considerations of convenience, reliability, cost and personal preference for one particular type of transport. Rarely do people consider the environmental effects of the form of transport. When a lorry or car is chosen, people are usually choosing the alternative which is environmentally the most damaging.

In contrast, eight per cent of kilometres travelled by people are by bus and seven per cent by rail. Rail carries 145 million tonnes of freight a year, but this is much less than the 108 585 million tonnes carried by road.

Motorway traffic jam.

If protection of the environment was one of the main deciding factors, then people would also consider:

Which form of transport

requires the least area of land to carry the same amount of goods or passengers? The less land taken, the less change to the environment is required.

makes the most efficient use of energy? Most fuels used in transport are non-renewable.

is the least polluting? Exhaust fumes can damage the environment. Noise pollution is also a problem in areas close to lines of transport.

Roadways

There are over 370 000 kilometres of road. Road building removes approximately 1000 hectares of open land a year. The amount of new road building could be reduced if more people travelled by public transport. Many common species of wildlife find safe homes on road verges.

One person travelling in a small car travels about 9 kilometres on a litre of fuel. A full bus carries a passenger the equivalent of 50 kilometres on a litre of fuel.

Petrol and diesel engines produce exhaust fumes. There are over 22 million vehicles on the roads of Britain producing polluting gases. Living close to a busy road can be very noisy.

Railways

There are about 16 500 kilometres of track in Britain. Railways require less space than roads to carry a similar number of people. They also require fewer raw materials. The sides of the track have encouraged a lot of wildlife since they were built. Some lineside areas have been designated **Sites of Special Scientific Interest** (SSSIs).

A passenger train can carry one person the equivalent of 55 kilometres on a litre of fuel. In large centres of population, trains are the only environmentally acceptable way of carrying large numbers of people to and from work. Freight carried by rail is 3.5 times more energy-efficient than that carried by road.

Twenty-five per cent of the track is electrified and no air pollution is caused along the route, although the power stations that generate the electricity cause pollution. Living close to a railway can be very noisy, but the noise is rarely constant.

For getting around, two forms of transport are often overlooked. Bicycles use the energy derived from a meal and create no pollution. Only small cycle tracks need to be made to enable a normal person to maintain an average speed of between 15 and 20 kilometres per hour, in safety, away from traffic. Walking is slower, but over short distances is an alternative. Both have the advantage of improving personal health and creating no noise.

In planning how to meet future demands for the movement of goods and people, conservationists say that the environment should be considered alongside convenience, reliability, cost and personal preference.

WHAT YOU CAN DO

1 Discuss with your family an energy conservation plan for your home and try to follow it.

2 If you were the Minister of Transport, how would you spend your money to cope with a 30 per cent increase in passenger and freight transport over the next 10 years?

3 Do you think that railways are the 'only environmentally acceptable way of moving large numbers of people to and from work' in large towns?

4 Lichens are good indicators of air pollution. The 'leafy' types require clean air to grow. Where the air is very heavily polluted very few types can grow. Carry out a transect from the road verge into a forest or woodland and plot the types that you find and how frequently they can be found.

4 Farming and food

Farmers have been very successful at producing the food we need. This section looks at how new farming techniques have changed the environment in ways that are criticised by many people, and how farming and conservation interests can be made more compatible.

Farming and the countryside

The countryside of Britain is mainly managed by farmers. There are over a quarter of a million farms and the average size of a farm is 50 hectares (equivalent to about 50 football pitches). Eighty per cent of Britain is farmland of one type or another. Only in a few areas of Scotland may the landscape be described as 'natural'. As well as farming, the countryside is used for building, recreation, mining, transport, training for the armed forces and forestry.

The landscape in some parts of Britain results from maintaining traditional farming methods.

All farming disturbs the environment. Over the centuries farming has created a countryside which many people find very attractive and which has provided a valuable variety of **habitats** for plants and animals.

Since 1945 technology has changed farming considerably and this has altered the appearance and **ecology** of the countryside.

Changes in farming

During the 1920s and 1930s, Britain imported 65 per cent of its food. This meant that during the Second World War it was difficult for Britain to get enough food and rationing was introduced which lasted until the early 1950s. Today, Europe can grow more than enough to meet its needs for key food products, in particular cereals and dairy products. What has made this possible?

Grain store — farming methods can now produce more than enough for our needs.

Government policies

Since 1945 it has been government policy to encourage farmers to produce more food. Before joining the European Community in 1973, the farmers were helped by:

- Deficiency payments – the government paid the farmers the difference between an agreed minimum price and the price they received at the market.

- Capital grants – money for new equipment, removal of hedges, draining the land and building new farm buildings.

Since 1973 the main support has come from:

- Intervention buying – The European Community buys farm produce when the price falls below an agreed figure and in theory sells it again when prices increase. However, surplus production meant that large stocks built up.

- Grants, including ones to help those farming difficult land such as uplands.

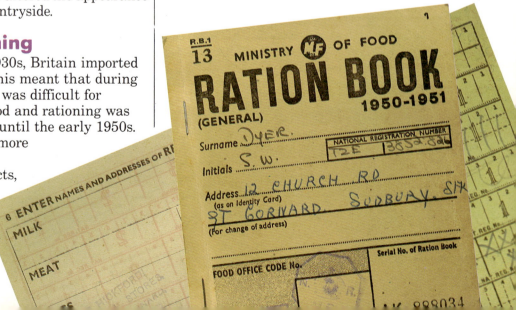

New farming methods

New methods of farming have led to huge increases in production.

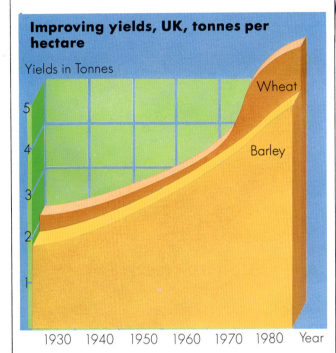

Improving yields, UK, tonnes per hectare

More powerful machines are able to do the work of many farm labourers. In East Anglia, for example, only one person is required to do the work that 10 people did in 1945.

Effect of fertilisers on wheat production in the UK

	Cost £ per ha	Yield tonnes per ha	Production cost £ per ha
NO FERTILISER	£479	1.69	£283
FERTILISED	£575	6.6	£87

Insecticides, fungicides and herbicides (often referred to collectively as pesticides) are sprayed on to crops to control or kill insects, fungi and weeds that could reduce food production or make the food unattractive. About 400 active chemicals are used in over 4000 different chemical products that have helped to guarantee a plentiful supply of food.

New ways of managing farm animals have greatly increased their **productivity**. Cows can now produce twice as much milk as in 1945. To provide the 12.7 billion eggs and 500 million chickens eaten each year in Britain, poultry are generally kept in intensive rearing units of up to 100 000 hens.

Animal welfare

Closely related to the environmental issues about modern agriculture, are the moral questions raised about the welfare of animals. In some modern farming systems animals are little more than production units in a factory. For example, 96 per cent of hens kept for egg production are housed in battery cages; in 1960 the figure was only 19 per cent.

FOR

Hens live in a warm, controlled environment, safe from the dangers and discomfort of life outdoors.

There is a regular supply of eggs.

Production costs are lower than for alternative methods.

AGAINST

It is not natural for hens to live in cramped cages where most natural behaviour is impossible.

Eggs from free range hens are in the shops all year round.

It is immoral to condemn hens to such conditions for the sake of a few pence on the price of an egg.

The consequences of change

What is the meaning of success?

In terms of food production, modern agriculture in Europe is a great success. It produces a regular supply of food at affordable prices in the quantities we need. However, critics say that the success has been achieved at a cost to the landscape, wildlife and farm animals. People are also worried about chemical **residues** left on food and the lack of choice as farmers concentrate production on fewer varieties.

Landscape changes

Changes to the landscape of the countryside have been caused by **arable** farming. Large fields are needed to make efficient use of the more powerful tractors, combine harvesters and other machines. Hedgerows, ponds and ditches are obstacles and many have been removed. By 1985, 175 000 of the 796 000 kilometres of hedges existing in 1974 had been removed. For example, by removing 2.5 kilometres of hedges from one farm in Devon, the amount of arable land was increased by 1.5 hectares and the amount of time needed to harvest the cereal crop was reduced by one-third.

Ecological changes

Changes in farming affect the wildlife interest of an area. Hedgerows, ponds and ditches are habitats for a variety of wildlife such as insects, birds and animals. When the habitat is removed, they have nowhere to shelter or feed. Over the last 40 years about half of Britain's wetlands have been drained to increase agricultural production.

Intensive farming in East Anglia.

Slurry (semi-liquid animal waste) must be disposed of carefully to avoid polluting nearby rivers and streams.

Plants and the use of fertilisers

The main elements a plant needs for healthy growth are:

Potassium (K) – Important for the growth of flowers, fruit and seeds. It increases a plant's ability to resist disease.

Nitrogen (N) – Encourages strong, healthy stems and leaves.

Phosphorus (P) – Essential for strong root development.

Fertilisers are used because most soils on farms do not contain enough of these essential elements that crops require for healthy growth and high productivity.

Modern farming techniques and fertilisers have reduced the wildlife interest of the countryside. Sixty thousand tonnes of nitrogen fertilisers were used in the 1930s. Today, 1.6 million tonnes are used. Meadows used for grazing animals used to be full of colourful wild flowers, but today only five per cent of these meadows remain. Nitrogen fertilisers encourage lush grasses which have taken over from the flowers.

Ploughing increases the amount of oxygen in the soil and this causes more nitrates to be produced. The problem is at its worst when well-established grasslands are ploughed up.

There has been a lot of publicity about the dangers of nitrates in drinking water. The European Community has set a limit on nitrate levels in drinking water at 50 parts per million. Water supplies in several parts of Britain regularly exceeded this in 1989.

Unlike fertilisers, pesticides are chemicals designed to kill pests. Most only control one or very few species, leaving others unharmed. However, by removing or contaminating part of a **food chain,** other species in the chain are likely to be affected.

Many chemicals used 20 years ago were not specific, ie they caused harm to a wide range of species. Organochlorine pesticides, such as **DDT** used in the 1950s and 1960s, caused a decline in numbers of birds of prey including the

Some people think that it is safer to drink bottled spring water than tap water.

Pollution of water supplies

Nitrates and phosphates are important nutrients for plants which grow in soil or in water. They are taken up in solution through the roots of the plant.

Nitrates are found naturally in the soil and in water but they also come from manure and are produced from nitrogen fertilisers by **micro-organisms** in the soil. Plants growing on land take up the nitrates that they need for growth and excess nitrates can be washed into the water supply.

Phosphates are also found naturally, in low concentrations. Excess phosphate comes largely from detergents and sewage. In water, phosphate is normally the nutrient in least supply and therefore limits the growth of plants.

Excess of nitrates and phosphates can be very damaging to the environment. Plants, especially unicellular algae, grow much more easily when excess phosphates or excess phosphates and nitrates are present and the ecology of the stream is upset. Excess plant growth may lead to the death of fish because of a lack of oxygen.

Where phosphate levels have been reduced this problem has been controlled. It is thought that reducing the amount of fertilisers used by farmers would reduce nitrates and would similarly ease the problem of excess plant growth. The problem of nitrates has, however, proved to be much more complicated.

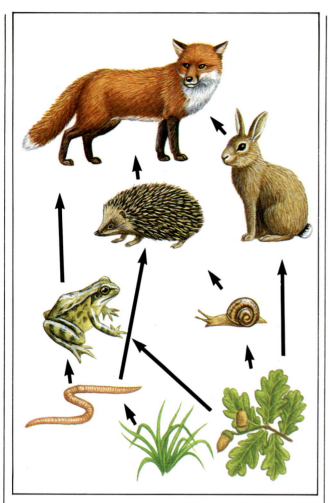

The connections between food chains link up to create a food web. Any change in the number (or feeding habits) of organisms at one link in a food web may affect many other plants and animals in the web.

sparrowhawk and peregrine falcon. Pigeons which ate seeds treated with the pesticides were eaten by peregrine falcons. The poison became established in the food chain. Once the cause of the problem was discovered, the chemicals were phased out. They were replaced with ones that break down more quickly and are not able to become established in food chains.

Chemicals are usually sprayed from long booms that stretch on either side of the tractor. Because some of the spray is very fine, it is easily carried away by the wind. Spray drift from herbicides may damage crops in adjoining fields and wild plants around fields. Insecticide spray drift can wipe out bees that are needed to pollinate plants. However, the high quality food demanded by supermarkets and shops cannot easily be produced without pesticides. If people were willing to buy fruit and vegetables with a few blemishes, then farmers could cut down on the use of chemicals.

Soil erosion

Soil erosion is increasing. Dry, light soils have been ploughed up, and **intensive** cultivation in other areas has reduced the **organic** content of the soil and damaged its structure. Wind blowing over dry, bare fields can carry away the fine topsoil. Water running downhill over bare fields removes the soil and can erode gullies. What can be removed in hours will take centuries to make again.

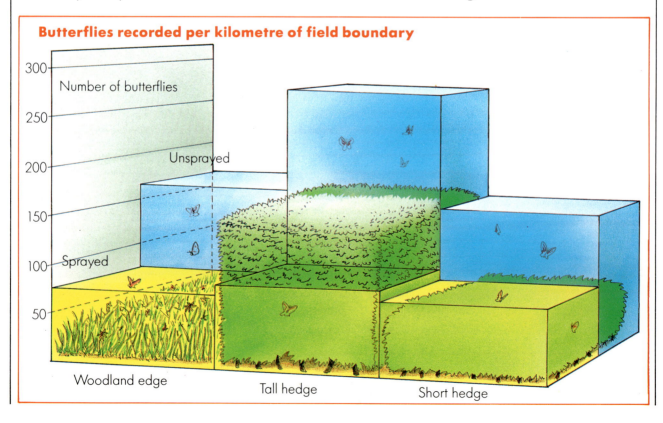

Finding the balance

Loss of wild plants and animals, soil erosion, pollution of streams and rivers, possible health hazards in food and keeping animals in intensive units; these are signs that we need to ask if agriculture has struck the right balance between modern technology and conservation. There is now pressure from **consumers** and from many farmers for new farming practices – as can be seen through the increasing sales of organically produced food and free-range eggs.

Farming and wildlife advisory groups

In 1969 a group of people with interests in farming, forestry and wildlife wanted to find out how advice could be given to farmers and other land managers on ways of maintaining wildlife on modern, well-run farms. From this initiative has developed a network of Farming and Wildlife Advisory Groups covering most of the country. These help farmers to conserve nature on their farms.

Reducing farm production

(See also Forestry and timber – Farm woodlands scheme).

The **European Community** is now encouraging farmers to cut down production of certain commodities. It is trying out a scheme which pays farmers up to £200 per hectare to take at least 20 per cent of their land out of arable production. In certain areas the **Countryside Commission** is offering extra payments to fund conservation work by the farmer.

Surpluses can also be reduced by farming the land less intensively. This would mean using less fertilisers and pesticides, or farming organically.

Organic farming

No type of farming is natural, but organic farming aims to protect the environment. Food is grown without the use of chemical fertilisers, pesticides or weedkillers. Instead, crop rotations break disease patterns and control weeds, and organic material is added to the soil. Yields in some cases match conventional farming, though even with good management, production is usually about 10 per cent lower. Organic farming could produce between 10–20 per cent of our food, although prices would be higher. The Soil Association sets standards for farming methods and the government has set up a register of organic food standards.

Organic farm produce. Alternative methods of farming are becoming more popular, but can they supply all the food we need?

CASE STUDY

Managing field margins for nature conservation

Since the 1940s, 40 per cent of the field margins in England and Wales have been lost as hedges and trees have been removed. An average arable farm still has about seventeen kilometres of field edges and these can be used less intensively for the benefit of wildlife. The Wildflower Project is a joint venture between the British Agrochemicals Association, the Cereals and Game Birds Research Project and the Nature Conservancy Council. It is looking at ways of managing field margins.

Intensive farming methods, fertilisers and pesticides have been largely responsible for the decline of many wild plants and animals including game birds, such as partridges, which live around arable fields. If the edges of the fields are farmed less intensively than the rest of the field, some of the wild plants may return. Seeds can remain in the ground for years, but never get the chance to grow. Plants not seen for 40 years have started to reappear and with them the insects on which the partridge chicks feed. Nature conservation benefits and the loss in production from a field of 15 hectares is only about 0.5 per cent.

Other developments

Interest in maintaining and improving the quality of the countryside environment is now so great that the conservation bodies, farmers and the agricultural industry are exploring ways of making modern farming and conservation compatible. There is not space to consider all the developments, but other examples can be followed up, including:

a) The development of new types of spray machinery which can be effective using 80 per cent less chemicals.
b) The use of new sprays which control only the pest causing the problem.
c) Using a pest's natural **predators** instead of chemical sprays, eg ladybirds to eat aphids.
d) Breeding hybrid varieties of crops that are more resistant to pests and diseases and do not need as much spraying as a result.
e) Genetically engineering cereals and other crops to act like peas and beans which fix their own nitrogen from the atmosphere. This would reduce the amount of fertilisers used.
f) Improving animal welfare.

Yellow rape fields are now a common sight in some parts of Britain. Plant breeders use this plant extensively for crop-improvement studies.

Who pays for conservation?

Farming is a commercial activity and for conservation to be acceptable to farmers it must enable them to continue earning a living. For farming to be acceptable to consumers, conservation will have to be taken into account. In **National Parks** and **Environmentally Sensitive Areas** where protection of the environment is very important, farmers can receive grants to farm in traditional ways which maintain the appearance and ecological interest of the landscape. In other areas, a site may be so valuable as a habitat for wildlife, that the farmer enters into a management agreement with a conservation body such as the **Nature Conservancy Council** to maintain it. Conservation bodies, most of which are charities, also buy land which is of special interest to them and manage it in such a way as to preserve its special qualities. But all this has to be paid for.

Where do you think the money should come from?

The outlook

The landscape and ecology of Britain's countryside are part of the national heritage that people can enjoy free of charge. The countryside also supports farming which is one of the country's biggest industries. Any changes in farming will lead to changes in the countryside and it is therefore important that the use of the countryside is planned carefully to reflect the variety of interests.

There are developments coming along which will continue to change farming. Biotechnology could affect agriculture as dramatically as developments in electronics during the past 20 years have affected industry. Plants containing **genes** from other plants will be able to resist diseases and pests without the use of chemical sprays. A cow which now is expected to produce between four and eight calves in its lifetime, will be able to produce seventeen or more. But are such developments morally acceptable? Biotechnology is a new issue to think about.

WHAT YOU CAN DO

Using old and new maps of an area near where you live, draw a map to show how much farmland has been lost to new buildings and roads and when they were built.

PAUSE FOR THOUGHT

1 Do you think it is right to cut down on food production in Europe when so many people in the world do not have enough to eat?

2 What effect do you think that a big growth in vegetarianism would have on farming in Britain?

5 Forestry and timber

Forests can serve many purposes including timber production, nature conservation, recreation, landscape improvement or to prevent soil erosion and flooding. This section considers some of the environmental issues in connection with timber production.

Why we need trees

In developed countries, like Britain, we have become very dependent upon wood. Homes are full of it, from doorframes to furniture. Newspapers, books, cardboard boxes and toilet rolls all began life as wood. Can you imagine life without wood? Trees and forests also provide habitats for wildlife, take in carbon dioxide, produce oxygen, protect the soil, and can improve the appearance of the landscape.

Many objects in our everyday lives are made from wood.

Sevenoaks in Kent is named after the oaks that grew there. This picture was taken in 1948 when they were mature trees.

Trees as crops

Trees are plants and like all plants they grow, mature and die. Whereas most plants grow and die back each year, trees take many years to grow to their full size. Some can live for hundreds of years, so it is hardly surprising that we sometimes forget they are plants at all. They seem to be permanent features of the landscape, much as are buildings and roads. However, to the forester, trees can be as much a crop as wheat is to the farmer. The main difference is the length of time between planting and harvesting.

Most of the wood produced in Britain comes from forests which have been specially planted for timber production. They have been planted on land which is not good quality farmland, usually infertile soils in upland areas. **Coniferous** trees are generally planted because they grow quickly and straight and are easier to process by timber mills. Sixty per cent of Britain's forests are planted with species of coniferous trees such as the sitka spruce, lodgepole pine and larch that do not grow there naturally.

Even a fast-growing conifer tree will take 50–60 years to grow large enough for cutting as timber. Broadleaved trees like oak grow much more slowly, and their wood is much harder and stronger.

Most of the forests created in Britain during this century have been planted like this coniferous forest on a hillside in the Spey Valley.

More trees are needed

(See also Using energy — the greenhouse effect).

Once Britain was extensively covered with forest, but by the end of the last century only five per cent of the land was wooded. Clearing land for farming and using wood for houses, furniture, ships, fuel (especially iron smelting) and tools, meant that little remained and timber had to be imported. During the First World War (1914–1918) it was very difficult to import wood and the government realised that it was dangerous to be over-reliant on timber supplies from overseas. In 1919 it decided to encourage the planting of more forests and set up the Forestry Commission so that there could be a reserve of trees should supplies from overseas be interrupted again.

Since then the amount of land under forest has increased to 10 per cent (2 100 000 hectares). This is still well below the 25 per cent average for other European countries and in 1988 the government confirmed its target of wanting 33 000 hectares of new planting a year.

Ways of encouraging people to plant trees

Without incentives, few investors would put their money into forestry. It is expensive to prepare the land and to plant the young trees. The forest must then be carefully managed to ensure that the trees remain healthy. It may be 50 years before any timber is sold.

To make it worthwhile, the government gives grants to encourage people to plant forests. For example, in 1989 grants of between £615 and £1005 per hectare were available for planting conifers and £975 to £1575 for broadleaved trees.

Small woodland in an agricultural area. As well as timber, the wood can provide shelter from high winds, fuel, an area for wildlife and help to reduce soil erosion.

Farm woodlands scheme

To help reduce production of certain farm products currently in excess, other uses of farmland are being encouraged. Farmers can apply for a grant to convert farmland into woodland. They can receive a grant to plant trees and an annual sum of between £30 and £190 per hectare for the next 30 years (1989 figure).

The aim of the scheme is to plant 36 000 hectares of land by 1991. As the land is fertile, it should be possible for farmers to plant a wider range of coniferous and **deciduous** trees than in upland plantations.

Forestry and the environment

When the Forestry Commission began its work in 1919, there was little interest in environmental protection. Its main task was to plant trees and start harvesting as soon as possible. It was not until later that concern for the environment became an issue.

Although conservationists are not opposed to forestry as such, conifer plantations are criticised by some people because:

- New forests are planted on moorlands and bogs, many of which are internationally important for communities of plants and animals that cannot survive in forests.
- They spoil the natural beauty of the landscape.
- Access to large areas of land is denied to the public.

- The local economies of some areas are suffering as there are few jobs available for local people.

The Royal Society for the Protection of Birds and the Forestry Commission have set up an observation site at Symonds Yat Rock on the River Wye where the public can watch a pair of peregrines on a cliff face.

Although the opposition has not changed the basic policy of planting more forests, it has meant that foresters have modified the way in which they manage the forests. Many are now popular with tourists and there are picnic sites, information centres and trails. It is also true that in some areas forestry has become the major employer.

Derwentwater in the Lake District. Opposition in the 1930s prevented this area from being planted with conifers. Today many people want to prevent forestry from spoiling exceptional environments.

CASE STUDY

Managing forests for profit and conservation

At Eskdalemuir in Dumfriesshire, the Economic Forestry Group is developing forests on 12 500 hectares of former sheep farming land. From the start in the 1970s, there has been close collaboration between local people, wildlife managers and the foresters. The aim was to find a satisfactory balance between all the interests represented.

The forestry team of 11 permanent staff and seven trainees is drawn from the local area. The four members of the wildlife team are required to live in the area and offer advice and support to local farmers as well. Amenities are being developed within the forest such as fishing, deer stalking and photography. These will bring visitors into the area and benefit hotels and bed and breakfast establishments. Local school pupils use the forest for their studies and also provide the forestry company with useful data.

Eskdalemuir led the way but today improvements in forest design are being explored by both nature conservationists and the forestry industry.

A pied flycatcher peeps out from a nesting box. Nesting sites can be created in forests to increase the number of birds. Birds are useful in that they help to keep down insects which can damage trees.

The forestry and wildlife teams work very closely together. Before any development took place, a soil map was prepared. From this it was decided which areas to leave unplanted for wildlife, where to site roads and drainage channels to fit in with the landscape and to select the types of trees which were best suited to the different conditions in the area.

Many of the people who have invested in the forest do not live in the area and need to be convinced that such expenditure is really necessary. They are encouraged to visit the area and see for themselves that such measures are actually protecting their investment, not wasting it.

Eskdalemuir in Scotland. By working with the local community and wildlife experts, the developing forest will provide a valuable resource, support for a variety of wildlife and provide an amenity for local people and visitors.

CASE STUDY

Dilemma in the Highlands

The conflict between forestry and conservation became most severe in the Flow Country of northern Scotland in 1988/9. This area of blanket bog covering 3900 square kilometres has remained almost unchanged for 6000 years. It is like a giant saturated sponge and is one of the wettest bogs in the world. It provides a habitat for plants and animals that is unique in Britain and very scarce in the rest of the world. The International Mire Conservation Group claims that its ecological value is equal to that of the Brazilian rain forest or the plains of the Serengeti in East Africa. Developers wanted to increase the area under forestry to 20 per cent and this brought about the conflict.

What the wildlife organisation says

The area should be protected because it is a unique habitat, supporting rare species of birds and containing many plants that are not found anywhere else.

The impact of forestry goes beyond the forestry boundary. Draining the land will change the movement of water and prevent the sphagnum moss from growing in areas outside the forest boundary.

The foresters' reply

If developers and conservationists plan the planting carefully, the damage to the wider environment can be kept to a minimum.

If the area under forest is increased, then it will be economic to process the timber locally instead of sending it to mills further south. This will create 2000 permanent local jobs.

A compromise plan allowing further planting has been accepted by the Nature Conservancy Council at the request of the Secretary of State for Scotland. The severity of the conflict has created a lot of bad feeling and shows how important it is to have a better way of planning where new forests should be sited.

Forestry indicative strategies

In Scotland, the Highlands, Strathclyde, Grampian and Borders regional authorities are trying to avoid conflict by working with foresters, farmers and conservationists to find the most suitable places for planting forests. Land already forested or unsuitable is plotted on a map. The remaining land is divided into three categories.

1 Preferred areas – the land is suitable for forestry and there is no major objection from conservationists or farmers.

2 Potential areas – the land is suitable for forestry but there are a few conservation or farming interests which will need to be settled before planting is allowed.

3 Sensitive areas – although the land is suitable, there would be a lot of opposition to forestry and resolving the issues would cost developers a lot of money and take a long time.

Such strategies are a more sensible way of planning the use of land because they help prevent conflict and make it possible to benefit from timber production without destroying valuable environments. Conservationists say that conflict could be avoided altogether if new planting took place on lowland farmland rather than on moorland.

The International timber trade and the environment

Although there has been extensive planting of new forests in Britain, about 90 per cent of the timber products used are imported. Imports are of **softwoods** from coniferous forests, **hardwoods** from **temperate forests** and hardwoods from tropical rain forests. As 75 per cent of the demand is for softwood, the bulk of imports are from the coniferous forests of Canada, Russia and Scandinavia.

The destruction of **natural forests** in the coniferous and tropical forest belts causes great concern. These forests are important sources of timber. People live and make their living in them, they help to control the climate, the composition of the atmosphere, flooding and soil erosion. They are **ecosystems** that have evolved over many thousands of years and can offer much more than wood. Many medicines and food crops used in the developed countries have their origins in forest plants, and scientists often need to return to wild varieties to breed new ones.

Coniferous forests

Twenty-one per cent of the world's forest resource is coniferous and the greatest demand is for wood from coniferous trees, most of which are found in the northern hemisphere. Much of the imported timber comes from clearing natural forest areas which are not always replanted. In that case all benefits of the forest are lost and this is a cause for concern. Some retailers such as Homebase now ensure that their timber only comes from areas that are replanted.

Tropical forests

There has been a lot of publicity about the destruction of the tropical rain forests which are found mainly in South America, West and Central Africa and South-East Asia. Every

Cultivation on the slopes of Mount Oku, Cameroon, as a result of forest clearance (above) demonstrates bad management of tropical forests where the land and tropical ecosystem is ruined for ever. Well managed forests like this one in Ghana, which has been selectively logged (below), can continue to provide resources.

year the area under forest declines by about 200 000 km², almost the same area as England and Scotland together.

Environmentally, these forests are very important. They protect the soil from the heat of the Sun and heavy rainfall, absorb carbon dioxide (see Using Energy), maintain the climate control flooding and erosion and have a greater variety of plants and animals than any other ecosystem on the land. They also have economic uses. They provide timber for local people and overseas customers, and plants are used in medicines and agriculture. Farmers also clear forests to grow food, but such land often becomes infertile very quickly. They are also the home for **traditional peoples** who have lived in the forest without damaging it for hundreds of years. The way in which the forest is exploited today is rarely compatible with its protection. Once cleared the Sun dries out the soil and rain washes away the soil nutrients. Within a few years the soil may be useless and the area may look more like a desert than a forest.

The majority of clearance is done by people moving into the areas to farm or collect fuel wood, but logging by timber companies is also threatening the forest. Local governments are faced with difficult decisions. The demand for timber is likely to increase at twice the rate of population growth across the entire world. Timber is one of the few resources they have to pay for necessities like oil, fertilisers and machinery. Rapid population growth in many of the countries means that there is a shortage of agricultural land and fuel wood, so people move into the forest and clear it.

Protecting the tropical forest

Creating forest reserves in which human activities are carefully controlled is one way of protecting the forest. Careful management and selective logging can help to maintain the rich diversity of animal-life and plant-life in the rain forests. Korup is a reserve in the Cameroons which has been established because it contains so many different species of plants and animals. Funds have to come from overseas agencies, or the country would not be able to afford to maintain it.

Countries often do not have enough money to protect their forests, so some ways of assisting them are being considered. One scheme is for conservation organisations in the richer countries to pay part of what the country owes the developed world for oil, vehicles, machines etc; in return the country protects an area of forest. The Timber Trade Federation is promoting a scheme to put a levy on all imports of tropical timber and return the money to the country of origin for conservation work.

In some areas the forest is being managed in such a way that timber is produced without destroying the environment or the livelihoods of people. This approach is being encouraged.

The outlook

The tropical forest can provide a constant supply of timber is only mature trees are felled. Trees grow much quicker than in the temperate zones and Brazilian mahogany is ready for cutting in only 25 years. But sensible management of commercial logging is only part of the problem. Non-damaging uses of the forest need to be found that will provide food and money for farmers without the forest having to be cleared.

WHAT YOU CAN DO

All paper and card can be recycled and this reduces the number of softwood trees that have to be cut down.
- Find out from where you can get recycled paper and its prices.
- Compare the cost of using recycled and non-recycled paper in your school.
- Design a scheme for collecting waste paper in the school and sending it to a recycling centre.
- Prepare a report for the headteacher explaining the costs and benefits of your school plan for 'saving trees'.

6 The extractive industry and building

This section examines the importance of aggregate (sand, gravel and crushed rock) in our industrialised society, the impact of excavations on the environment and the ways in which old workings can be used.

(See also Sources of Energy — open cast coal mining).

While few people would welcome the opening of a pit close to where they live, most are happy to enjoy the benefits that minerals such as sand and gravel bring.

Minerals are needed for houses, roads, hospitals, glass, etc. Our way of life depends on them.

Workings often attract an interesting variety of wildlife. Old workings can be developed as conservation or recreation areas.

There are 18.7 million hectares of agricultural land and the amount used for excavation is tiny. Land can be returned to agricultural use when the site is worked out.

Excavation provides employment for local people and supports the local economy.

Excavation can spoil the landscape and destroy or disturb the ecology of an area that may have taken hundreds of years to evolve.

About 1750 hectares of valuable agricultural land are taken a year.

Excavation creates noise, dust and extra traffic on the roads. It is unpleasant for local people.

Aggregate extraction

Annual production is around 300 million tonnes, of which 45 per cent is sand and gravel and 55 per cent crushed rock. It is bulky but inexpensive and transport can increase its price considerably. As a result, there is great pressure to excavate resources which are close to urban areas where most building takes place. These are the same areas where there is also a great demand for land for food production, roads, factories, houses and recreation. Finding an acceptable balance between these competing uses is the responsibility of the local planning authority which must give planning permission before any new excavation can begin. It can also enforce conditions about how the land is to be restored once the site is exhausted.

A working gravel pit. Minerals are needed for houses, roads etc, but their excavation changes the landscape and ecology.

Excavating the sea bed

Sand and gravel being off-loaded from a dredger.

Companies are also dredging sand and gravel from the sea bed. About 16 million tonnes of sand and gravel are taken a year, reducing the amount of land needed by 300 hectares. Marine sand and gravel is usually used at coastal or river sites. For example, 450 000 tonnes were used in the Thames Barrier. The Channel Tunnel construction takes about 8000 tonnes a day from the Goodwin Sands. Although this reduces the amount of land required for excavation, dredging may cause extra erosion along the coast. Part of the problem is that no one really knows what the effect will be.

Restoring the land

The main way of minimising the impact of excavation on the local environment has been to return the land to its former use once the site is worked out. About half the workings that are restored are returned to agriculture, but this is now less important as the European Community wants to cut back on production of certain agricultural items. Some sites are developed for recreation purposes, especially water sports like sailing and water skiing. There is also increasing interest in conserving old quarries and spoil heaps as nature reserves or creating new nature conservation areas from old workings. The Nature Conservancy Council has made 75 of them Sites of Special Scientific Interest (SSSIs) because they are so rich in wildlife.

In the past there was a temptation for some extraction companies to take the cheap alternative of just leaving land alone and letting nature take its course. However, the wildlife interest of these sites may not be great. It is better to develop and manage a nature conservation area to keep a variety of habitats. What can be done is shown by a case study of what happened at Amwell in the Lea Valley in Hertfordshire.

CASE STUDY

Restoration: Amwell Wildlife Reserve

The Amwell site was once an area of meadows separated by ditches lined with pollarded willows. In 1973, Hertfordshire County Council gave permission to the RMC Group to extract sand and gravel as long as the land was restored for 'low intensity recreational use'. By 1988, 1.9 million tonnes had been excavated and the old working filled with water.

In 1983 restoration of some of the area that had been worked began. The company worked with local wildlife experts and volunteers on an ambitious plan to turn 43 hectares of the site into a wildlife reserve. The banks of the lake were made longer by building spits, bays and islands. This provided more space for water birds to breed. Nest boxes were put up to encourage more birds to nest there, native trees were planted to attract more birds and insects, and the gradients of the shore reduced to provide more shallow water. New habitats have been created, in one case by importing coal ash from a power station to create a wet-fen.

Today, 186 species of birds have been recorded there, 278 species of flowering plants and 16 species of dragonfly. The dragonflies alone make it eligible for designation by the Nature Conservancy Council as a Site of Special Scientific Interest. It has won many conservation awards.

Only a few sites have been developed in this way, but they provide a safe haven for wildlife and a valuable public amenity.

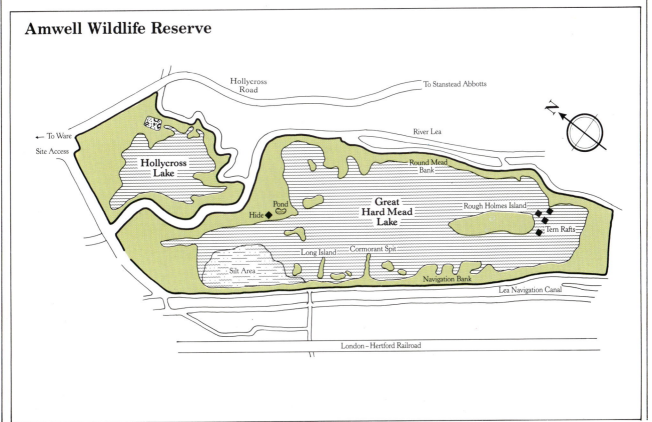

Amwell Wildlife Reserve

CASE STUDY

Protecting the environment – public pressure

In 1987, a sand and gravel company asked for planning permission to extract sand and gravel from a 53 hectare site near the village of Sutton Saint Nicholas in Herefordshire. The area covers good agricultural land and is a rural area with high landscape value. Local people were opposed to the development and set about trying to stop it. The case study shows that public pressure can be effective, although it also raises the question 'From where do we obtain the materials for new roads, houses, factories, etc?'

A company seeks planning permission to develop the site.

The Parish Council meets and forms Sutton Defence Force.

An application is received from another company.

A public meeting is held in Hereford to generate support for the campaign against the development. Every household in the area is sent leaflets, two more public meetings are held and local councillors and Members of Parliament lobbied to gain their support.

The District Council meets and recommends rejection of the planning applications. The Group now tries to persuade the County planners with an 800-strong petition and organised public demonstrations.

Funds are raised for the fight by selling pen and ink drawings of the area by a local artist.

A glossy brochure outlining the reasons for opposition is sent to all councillors on the planning committee of the County Council.

The planning committee defers a decision until the planning officers have had time to negotiate with the developers.

The companies produce an amended plan and resubmit it. They point out that the government requires all local authorities to have 10 years supply of sand and gravel available in any one year and Hereford and Worcester only have four.

The County Council rejects the applications, not on environmental grounds, but because the local road will not stand up to the traffic. Road improvements would cost half a million pounds.

The companies decide to pull out.

All is quiet again.

WHAT YOU CAN DO

1 You live two kilometres from a small village which has no by-pass. It is a major routeway for heavy lorries and holiday traffic which create constant traffic congestion, noise and dirt in the village. A by-pass is proposed but it requires sand and gravel from a new pit at the end of your garden. What are your views on this? Would they be different if you lived in the village?

2 What other raw materials are excavated and what are they used for? Use a geological map to find out where the rocks are found.

7 Industry and the environment

Industry is a major employer in developed countries and the products that it makes have improved the standard of living. It also uses resources, creates waste and can damage wild places. This section looks at the impact of industry on the environment and how problems are being solved.

In the past industry did not pay much attention to its impact on the environment, but any damage was generally restricted to the local area. Today the industrial process and the products of industry, such as cars, are so widespread that industrial activities are threatening the global environment.

Types of industry

Primary industries
Farming, forestry and the extractive industries such as mining and quarrying.

Secondary industries
Industries that process raw materials and manufacture goods from them such as the chemical, iron and steel, clothing, furniture and car industries.

Tertiary industries
Industries that provide services for people and other industries including tourism, banking, transport and shops.

Changes in industry

The industrial structure of Britain has changed considerably over the past 20 years. Many of the original manufacturing industries such as ship building have declined. In other industries there have been huge rises in productivity so that fewer employees are needed. In the future even more jobs could be automated as computers become more powerful. With greater wealth and more free time, how will people be occupied? (See Tourism, recreation and enjoyment.)

Factories in Sheffield, 1885 — the environment was not the industry's first consideration.

Percentage of workforce in UK employed in different types of industry

	1963	1973	1983
Agriculture	3	2	2
Mining	3	2	2
Manufacturing	37	35	26
*Construction and utilities	9	8	6
Services	48	53	64

*eg the building, electricity and gas supply industries

Person hours to produce one ton of liquid steel

(chart showing decline from ~12 person hours in 1980 to low values by 1990)

Making way for new industry, British Steel demolishes a blast furnace at its Corby works (above) following the closure of iron and steel making in 1980. The works still operates and is the largest manufacturer of hot-finished electrically welded steel tubes in Europe. Redeveloped blast furnace site as it is today (below).

Environmental consequences of industrial development

From the manufacturing process

When raw materials are processed, energy is used and this can contribute to air pollution (see Using energy). Many processes use dangerous chemicals which, if allowed to get into the environment, can cause a lot of damage.

Natural systems are nature's way of turning waste into raw materials. The dead tree rots and is broken down by fungi, insects and bacteria until the nutrients it contains can once again be used by growing plants. Some of the waste from the production and use of industrial products can be recycled by natural processes, but only if these systems are not overloaded.

Industrial accidents

In 1984 there was an explosion at the Union Carbide factory in Bhopal. A cloud of very poisonous methyl isocyanate gas engulfed the surrounding area where thousands of people lived. About 2500 people died almost immediately. Even four years later, people were still dying at the rate of one a day. More than half a million people have been affected and many will suffer for the rest of their lives.

Should all industrial activities be 100 per cent safe whatever the cost? What is an acceptable risk?

From waste disposal

Getting rid of unwanted waste is an added cost to industry and the authorities have to decide what level of pollution from waste is acceptable. Standards are not the same in all countries and some industrialists say that this enables countries with fewer regulations to produce goods more cheaply.

The difficulty of proving damage

Polychlorinated biphenyls (PCBs) are used in electrical equipment, plastics and flame retardants. They are very toxic and if they get into the environment, they do not decay but become established in food chains and then build up in animal (including human) and plant tissue. One of the effects of the chemicals is to reduce the effectiveness of the body's immune system and make people and animals more prone to disease. They are so dangerous that no new uses are being allowed, but there is so much in old equipment that hundreds of tonnes still need to be disposed of safely. There were five tonnes of PCBs in transformers on Piper Alpha when it caught fire. They are unaccounted for, and may still be sealed in the transformers now lying on the sea bed. Five tonnes is equal to the total amount of PCBs getting into the North Sea a year.

PCBs can be disposed of safely by burning at temperatures of over 1100 degrees Celsius, but maintaining these temperatures for the 20 seconds required is very difficult. If they are not burnt properly, they become highly poisonous dioxins and furans which can cause cancer. An incinerator at Bonnybridge in Scotland, owned by Rechem, was found to have dropped to 850 degrees Celsius on several occasions. Local people claimed in court that the fumes from the plant were

Ocean incineration and harassment by Greenpeace.

responsible for numerous cattle deaths, similar birth defects in two children and an increase in cancer rates but they could not prove any link with the incinerator.

It is usually difficult to prove what has caused environmental damage because there are so many different factors at work and it is almost impossible to sort out the effects of just one of them.

Incineration now takes place at sea. Sixty-five nations have signed the Convention on the Prevention of Marine Pollution by Dumping of Wastes and other Matter (1972) agreeing to ban ocean incineration by 1994 unless it can be proved to be safe. This is a major change – usually the conservationist has to prove that a process damages the environment.

From the manufactured product

The sheer quantity of some of the manufactured products in use is a threat to the environment.

Example: Chlorofluorocarbons (CFCs) and the ozone layer: Ozone is a form of oxygen found in the **stratosphere** that filters out 99 per cent of the sun's harmful ultraviolet radiation. Even a one per cent increase in ultraviolet radiation at the Earth's surface can damage plant growth and lead to an increase in skin cancers and cataracts which cause blindness. In the 1980s researchers were alarmed to find that the ozone layer became very thin in winter over Antarctica. In 1987 there was no ozone over an area of sky as large as the USA. The 'ozone hole' had arrived. The layer over the North Pole is now also subject to seasonal thinning.

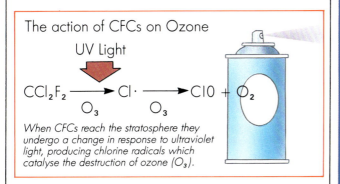

The action of CFCs on Ozone

$$CCl_2F_2 \xrightarrow{UV Light} Cl\cdot \xrightarrow{O_3} ClO \xrightarrow{O_3} + O_2$$

When CFCs reach the stratosphere they undergo a change in response to ultraviolet light, producing chlorine radicals which catalyse the destruction of ozone (O_3).

This damage is being caused by a group of chemicals known as CFCs. They have been widely used in aerosols, refrigerators and air conditioning units, styrofoam cartons for the food industry and for cleaning electronic components. When released into the atmosphere CFCs do not break up. They accumulate and are eventually carried above the ozone layer where they are broken down by the sun's ultra-violet radiation. As they break down a special form of chlorine is released which converts the ozone back to oxygen. Even if CFCs were banned from tomorrow, it would take 50 years for the ozone layer to return to the condition it was in before ozone-depleting chemicals were available.

Finding the balance

Using resources efficiently cuts down on waste and pollution. Improved techniques for burning fossil fuels, for example, have reduced emissions of sulphur dioxide by 25 per cent in Europe since 1978, although emissions are increasing again as industry expands.

Design for re-use or recycling

Industrial products can be designed so that they can be easily re-used or recycled. Over the last 20 years, an increasing number of products have been designed to be 'disposable', in other words, once they are used they are thrown away. The bottle which was once returned to the shop has been replaced by a throw-away plastic one. Even materials that can easily be recycled are thrown away. This adds to the mountains of rubbish for which it is increasingly difficult to find an equivalent hole to put it in.

Glass Recycling

Glass is completely recyclable. Yet every year in Britain, 1.5 million tonnes of it are thrown away. To make one tonne of new glass requires either 12 tonnes of raw materials which have to be dug out of the ground, therefore contributing to the damage of the environment – or one tonne of old glass. Each tonne of old glass used saves 135 litres of fuel, thereby reducing pollution and conserving a non-renewable resource. The Glass Manufacturers' Association says that it will take all the old glass it can get because it makes glass production much cheaper.

Bottle banks have become the accepted way of recycling glass and 1200 towns now have the familiar skips which are used by six million people a week. The broken glass (cullet) fetches between £20 and £30 per tonne, and the profits are usually given to local charities. People, industry and the environment benefit. However, only 14 per cent of the glass used in Britain gets recycled compared with 37 per cent in Germany, 50 per cent in Switzerland and 29 per cent in Europe as a whole.

There is an alternative which would save even more energy and cause less pollution. Bottles can be returned and re-used. What do you think the bottle manufacturers would think of that idea?

Design for the environment Some companies are now giving a high priority to designing products that cause minimum damage to the environment, both when they are manufactured and when they are used by the consumer.

Environment friendly products are becoming popular and more easily obtainable.

In West Germany, where consumers are very concerned about the damaging effects of their lifestyles on the environment, companies are responding by producing 'green' products. AEG produces a range of domestic appliances such as washing machines, dishwashers, vacuum cleaners and refrigerators which have been designed 'with the emphasis always on economy and ecology as much as on performance'. These machines all use the latest technology. For example, load sensors in the washing machines relate the water required to type and size of load, rather than treating all loads in the same way.

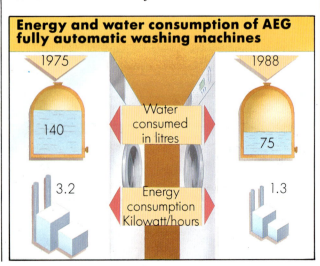

Energy and water consumption of AEG fully automatic washing machines

Public opinion

The interest in protecting the environment is reflected in the growing demand for information about how to live without destroying the environment. In 1988 a book called 'The Green Consumer Guide', written by John Elkington and Julia Hailes and published by Victor Gollancz Ltd, was published. This gave details of 'environment friendly' products and practical advice on how to live more ecologically. It had sold a quarter of a million copies by the middle of 1989.

Legislation for the environment: Laws must be enforced to help protect the environment. The Clean Air Act (1956) was very effective at reducing the 2.5 million tonnes of smoke that were put into the air in Britain every year. The story of the Control of Pollution Act (1974) is not so good. In 1988 only 23 of the 79 waste disposal authorities had sent waste disposal plans to the Department of the Environment, even though the act required them to do so. The European Community is increasingly requiring member countries to achieve higher environmental standards.

International agreements: Many environmental problems are international and require international agreements. Nations can be brought together by an international organisation such as the United Nations Environment Programme. In 1979, 30 countries signed an agreement to reduce their emissions of sulphur dioxide. In 1985 they fixed a reduction of 30 per cent to aim for, creating what has become known as 'The 30% Club'. In 1987 the world's first treaty on CFC consumption was signed in Montreal. This required the countries involved to reduce their consumption by 50 per cent before 1990.

The outlook

The changing attitudes towards environmental protection in industry, government and among individuals are very encouraging. There is a lot of work to be done, but it is impossible to solve all the problems at once. Careful monitoring of the environment can inform decision-makers about which problems should be given the highest priority. The United Nations Environment Programme set up the Global Environment Monitoring System to collect the data that the experts need.

CASE STUDY

Controlling pollution – the iron and steel industry

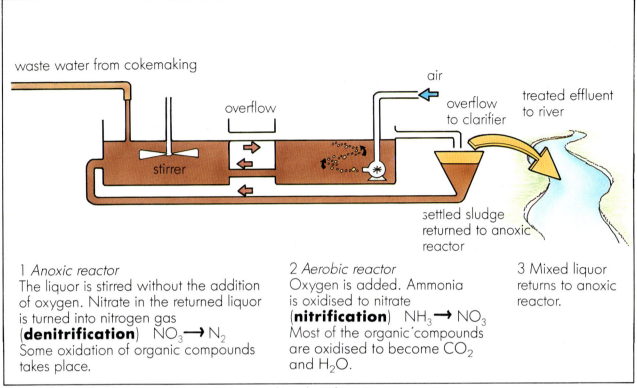

1 *Anoxic reactor*
The liquor is stirred without the addition of oxygen. Nitrate in the returned liquor is turned into nitrogen gas (**denitrification**) $NO_3 \rightarrow N_2$
Some oxidation of organic compounds takes place.

2 *Aerobic reactor*
Oxygen is added. Ammonia is oxidised to nitrate (**nitrification**) $NH_3 \rightarrow NO_3$
Most of the organic compounds are oxidised to become CO_2 and H_2O.

3 Mixed liquor returns to anoxic reactor.

Pollution control at Orgreave. Ammonia is turned into harmless nitrogen gas.

The manufacture of iron and steel uses a lot of energy, chemicals and water. Harmful by-products are produced which are found in the water used in the processes and running off the site. If allowed to flow into streams these by-products can kill fish and other living things. That used to happen 70 years ago, but things have improved greatly since then.

Yorkshire Water wanted to improve the quality of the River Rother. To do that British Steel had to reduce the amount of water pollution from its coke works at Orgreave (coal is turned into coke in huge ovens and then mixed with iron ore in a blast furnace to make iron). One of the most difficult pollutants to control was ammonia. An elaborate processing plant has been built which turns most of the ammonia into harmless nitrogen gas (nitrogen makes up 78 per cent of the air we breathe). Ammonia in the waste water has decreased from 100–150 milligrams per litre to between one and five milligrams per litre, well below the standard of 50 milligrams per litre set by Yorkshire Water. Organic compounds are another cause of pollution in the water and these are oxidised to carbon dioxide and water.

Pollution control has been achieved by a combination of legislation, public demands for higher standards and the use of new technologies.

Many large industries such as British Steel are responding positively to environmental matters as this example illustrates.

WHAT YOU CAN DO

1 It can be very interesting to know what other people think about environmental issues and what they would do to protect the environment. Working in groups, prepare some questions and conduct your own environmental public opinion poll in school. Write up your conclusions.

2 Which of the following do you consider to be a necessity and which a luxury? What do you think that people would have said 50 years ago?

☐ washing machine ☐ car ☐ dishwasher
☐ fitted carpets ☐ stereo ☐ television
☐ central heating ☐ bicycle ☐ holiday

3 Keep a log of what is thrown out daily from your home under these headings: can be reused; can be recycled; hazardous; no use. Which items, if any, do you take for recycling?

8 The urban environment

Most people in Britain today live in towns. This section looks at environmental problems and how industry, government, local authorities and community groups are trying to improve the urban environment.

The growth of towns

The growth of the major towns and cities in Britain is closely linked to the growth of the manufacturing industry and the rise in population over the last 200 years or so. Shops, offices and public buildings were built in the centre of towns because this was the easiest place for people to get to. Around the centre, factories and terraced houses were built. Conditions for many people were atrocious as the houses were often badly built, crammed together and lacked adequate sanitation. Beyond this, were the large houses of the richer factory owners, traders and business people, and beyond them, the countryside.

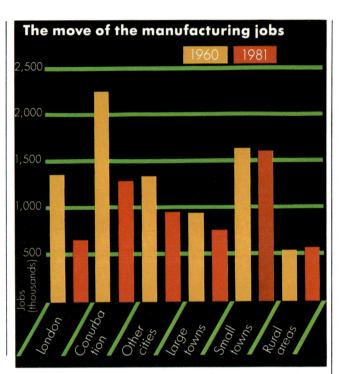

Slum dwelling in London at the turn of the century.

Today, these old areas of development form the inner city. The countryside beyond the Victorian 'mansions' has become a suburbia of semi-detached houses with gardens, schools, shops, etc. Some of the industries in the town have either closed down or moved to new industrial estates on the edges of towns. The inner city was regarded as out of date and was neglected along with the people who lived there.

Civic pride — Bradford Town Hall at night.

The environmental consequences of change

Urban environments

The volume of human activities in urban areas has a major impact on the environment. The ground is covered with buildings, tarmac and concrete. The climate is generally warmer and the air, soil and water courses more polluted. There is less open space for wildlife although some species such as foxes, starlings and pigeons have adapted very well to urban conditions. Parks, school grounds and suburban gardens can produce a variety of habitats especially if managed as wildlife areas.

High rise flats in London. Are these a suitable replacement for the slums of the last century?

New town developments

Many people want to have easy access to the countryside. One of the aims of new towns, such as Peterlee in County Durham or Welwyn Garden City in Hertfordshire, was to provide rural area living conditions with all the advantages of the town. Developers are now wanting to build mini-towns in south-east England to provide 200 000 extra homes that are needed but not catered for in any of the local plans. However, such developments take up more open space and attract money that could be spent on improving areas in the inner city.

Urban sprawl

As more building takes place around cities and in smaller towns, open space is lost and the amount of countryside between one town and the next is reduced. Between 1933 and 1963, an average of 26 000 hectares a year were lost to urban development. To maintain agricultural production, farming has had to become more intensive (see Farming and food) and there is more pressure on existing open space for leisure and recreation activities (see Tourism, recreation and enjoyment).

Milton Keynes is a new town designed for the twentieth century.

Out-of-town shopping centre in Basingstoke.

Before widespread car ownership, most people bought their everyday needs at local shops and went to the town centre for their major purchases such as furniture and clothes. Today, new shopping centres are being built outside the towns. Retail companies want to build 600 more out-of-town shopping centres. In America 54 per cent of shopping is done at out-of-town shopping centres and this has reduced the importance of town centres as shopping areas.

Inner city decline

The centres of the towns have attracted new investment in shopping schemes and office developments, but the people and the environment of the inner city around the centre have often been neglected. These areas often have social problems and the poor environment is partly responsible. Inner cities contain almost 200 000 hectares of waste land, an area equivalent to twice the size of Leeds.

Improving the cities

The inner cities are the areas most in need of renovation, and there are a number of programmes designed to improve the environmental and economic conditions. Community groups, private industry, the local authority and the government are all involved. They recognise the importance of creating open spaces and conservation areas alongside improving houses and creating more jobs. In some areas the improvements have been so successful that people are moving back into the city and causing house prices to rise beyond what local people can afford. All improvements can also affect other aspects of the environment. For example, energy and raw materials will be used, waste and pollution created and traffic will increase.

The London Docklands before redevelopment (above). Government action and private investment have worked together to transform the area (right).

Government action: The government has set up an Urban Programme and contributes 75 per cent of the cost of projects that tackle environmental and social problems in inner cities. Urban Development Corporations have been set up to improve derelict areas such as the London Docklands. The area has been transformed, but schemes are criticised because the wishes of local government and local people are not adequately catered for.

Local government: Local governments are keen to attract development back into the cities and one way of doing this is by improving the quality of the environment. Old buildings are cleaned and improved, new shopping malls built, vehicles removed from shopping streets, bus and cycle lanes created and support given to theatres and other cultural activities. There is also a movement to 'green' the cities with tree planting schemes, gardens and plants and bushes planted on road verges, etc. Halifax, one of the oldest industrial towns of Yorkshire, has received an award for being one of the most pleasant towns in Britain in which to live.

Industry: The industrial development of towns during the last century went hand in hand with the growth of the railways. The railways provided transport for raw materials, manufactured goods and people. During the twentieth century the railways have contracted, and road transport now carries 80 per cent of industrial goods. The railways have been modernised and many of the sidings, goods yards and buildings are not needed any more. Some have become valuable open space for wildlife and people. Local residents in Islington have been able to enjoy Gillespie Park which was developed on land belonging to British Rail. Now that it is having to sell the land it does not need, such areas are likely to be lost.

CASE STUDY

Urban regeneration

British Rail has a great deal of property and many buildings in run-down inner city areas. By working with local communities to improve the appearance of the railway and to find new uses for disused buildings, BR is helping to improve the dull urban landscape and to revitalise the fabric of community life.

Twenty years ago, BR, like many owners of property, modernised by knocking down the old and building new. Today, attitudes have changed; while some new building continues, attractive old stations are carefully refurbished and given a new lease of life. Others not required for the railway are converted to new uses. It is a carefully designed blending of old with new.

Railway viaduct arches have always attracted small businesses looking for cheaper premises. Unfortunately, in many cases their activities created eyesores and did little to enhance the urban environment. Working with local authorities and voluntary groups, British Rail has a programme of shared-cost schemes to refurbish arches, clean viaduct brickwork and create new facilities that establish attractive, affordable premises for a wide variety of commercial uses – from bakers to pop recording studios! So great are the improvements, that some of the arch refurbishments have won environmental awards.

Kirkgate arch redevelopment, Leeds.

With the support of special government grants for urban renewal, Brixton Station in south London and Liverpool's Lime Street Station – among many others – have been environmentally improved, and even whole rail 'corridors' through major cities are being tackled. By upgrading these 'gateways' to inner city areas, visitors get a better first impression of the area, residents gain a better working and living environment and businessmen are encouraged to invest in new development for a brighter future.

Community action: Most urban redevelopment has taken place without involving local people. The developers have maintained that it is too complicated to be entrusted to ordinary people. This is an attitude that has been criticised by Prince Charles, who has given a lot of support to a movement known as Community Architecture. It starts from the principle that 'the built environment works better if the people who use it are directly and actively involved in its creation and management'.

City farm projects. Communities work towards improving the inner city environment.

There is now a very strong community movement working towards improving the inner city environment. Urban Wildlife Groups are developing wild areas in towns for the benefit of wildlife and local people. Think Green, Groundwork Trusts, City Farms, and Architectural Workshops are all examples of the many groups that work with the communities to protect and improve the environment.

Ecological guidelines for urban development and planning

Improving the environment is a feature of most inner city development plans. The Nature Conservancy Council has produced guidelines to help developers include nature conservation. They contain the following advice:

1 Avoid pollution of soil, air and water.

2 Avoid hard surfaces wherever possible. Surface water should be channelled into ponds or soakaways where possible, not watercourses.

3 Habitats with a long history should be identified and protected.

4 Green spaces should be linked by green corridors so that plant and animal communities do not become isolated.

5 Large areas of green space are more valuable than an equivalent area of smaller isolated ones.

6 Every effort should be made to create a variety of habitats.

7 In heavily built up areas, window boxes, climbing plants, roosting sites, and roof gardens can be designed into buildings.

8 When landscaping areas, use native species as far as possible.

Britain needs to make its towns attractive and enjoyable places in which to live or there will be demands for yet more of the countryside to be built on. A lot of money is being spent, although not all people agree that it is enough or spent on the right things.

WHAT YOU CAN DO

Working in groups of three, explore your local environment. Mark on a map those areas or buildings which you dislike and like and explain why. Alternatively, draw some of the places and mark on the features which you like and dislike. Suggest ways in which you think your local environment could be improved.

9 Tourism, recreation and enjoyment

There is an increasing demand for leisure and tourist facilities in the countryside. This section examines how new facilities can be provided without spoiling the environment.

A growth industry

Providing for tourism and recreation has become a major industry in Britain. Since 1974, the number of visitors to Britain has risen from 8.5 million to 13.7 million. British people too are tourists in their own country more than before—the numbers have gone up by 20 per cent during the last 10 years. A survey by the Countryside Commission in 1984 showed that 18 million people made a trip into the countryside on a typical summer Sunday—75 per cent of the trips by car. Although there are about 200 000 kilometres of public rights of way in England and Wales (there is access to most open space in Scotland), people tend to go to well-known beauty spots. Snowdon is climbed by 400 000 people a year, while a few kilometres away there are hills where few people are to be seen.

Causes of the change

People have more money and more time for leisure activities. The improved road network has made the countryside more accessible. For example, the motorways put 25 million people within a three-hour drive of the Lake District, one of the most popular national parks.

People are also encouraged to travel more into the countryside. In 1968 the Countryside Commission and the Countryside Commission for Scotland were set up to 'enhance the natural beauty of the countryside and to help people enjoy it'. They have encouraged many developments such as open days on farms, and have created over 2500 kilometres of long distance footpaths. Greater interest in health has led to a growth in outdoor pursuits which often take place in the countryside.

Map of Britain showing Areas of Outstanding Natural Beauty (National Scenic Areas in Scotland), National Parks and the motorway network.

The consequences

In the countryside, tourism and recreation have to exist alongside other activities such as farming and forestry. The impact of new developments such as theme parks, hotels and holiday villages and millions of visitors can spoil the appearance of the countryside, disrupt farming, damage wildlife areas, increase pollution and (especially in forests) be a fire risk.

The Pennine Way long distance footpath.

The impact of recreation on wildlife

IMPACT	ACTIVITY
Disturbance to nesting birds:	
Cliff breeding eg auks, peregrine, chough	Climbing, sub-aqua, canoeing, pleasure boats
Moorland eg dunlin, grey plover, raptors	Public access
Woodland eg nightjar	Orienteering, public access
Beaches eg little tern	Public access
Waterside eg wildfowl	Windsurfing, angling
Lead poisoning in swans and wildfowl	Angling, wildfowling
Disturbance to bats	Caving, canal boats (bats live in the tunnels)
Damage to moorland	Long-distance footpaths, motor sports
Damage to sand dunes	Motor sports, beach access
Damage to limestone caves	Caving

The impact of visitors

The most popular areas for walking are upland areas. The footsteps of thousands of people toiling up a hill can wear away the grass that holds the soil in place. Heavy rains wash away the soil and create ugly gullies. Along the Lyke Wake Walk in the North York Moors, 20 000 walkers a year have compressed the peat from 2.5 metres thick to less than half a metre. The path has become increasingly boggy and detours are made. The path is now 400 metres wide! Paths are also damaged by horses, motor cycles and four wheel drive vehicles.

Although visitors may bring much needed income to a community, they can also cause much disturbance. Fowey in Cornwall is a beautiful village at the mouth of the River Fowey. Over 50 per cent of the homes are owned by people who do not live in the village. For much of the year they are empty and there is little benefit to the local economy.

Traffic chaos in a small village causes much disturbance.

This footpath in Trow Gill in the Yorkshire Dales has been eroded away by the feet of many walkers.

Finding the balance

In a survey undertaken in 1982, people were asked what things contributed most to the quality of life. An attractive countryside came second in the list after safe streets. How can the increasing demand for tourism and recreation in the countryside be met without causing problems?

WHAT YOU CAN DO

Using other trail guides as an example, work out a short trail and produce a trail guide to help visitors learn more about interesting places in your local area. Consider what effect a lot of visitors using the trail would have on local people and the environment.

CASE STUDY

Green tourism in Aberfeldy: a community approach

Aberfeldy is a small town near Loch Tay to the north west of Perth with a population of about 1600. Three thousand people live in the surrounding hills and valleys and regularly visit the town for their shopping and entertainment. The area is very beautiful and rich in wildlife. It is listed as an Environmentally Sensitive Area. It attracts a lot of visitors. The local community has set up LOCUS (LOCal focUS). It has produced a plan which should help visitors to enjoy the area more, while at the same time benefiting the local community and protecting the environment.

LOCUS marked on a map all the attractions of the area that visitors might enjoy, eg good walks in beautiful scenery, archaeological sites, farming, white water canoeing and wildlife. Trails linking interesting places were prepared on several themes including farming, conservation, local crafts and forestry. The farm trail, for example, visits a dairy farm, a sheep farm, an organic farm, a smallholding (small farm), a deer park and a heavy horses centre. All the trails start and finish in the centre of Aberfeldy where an information centre has been converted from a redundant church.

The economic and environmental advantages of the trails are:
- Local people can develop facilities for the visitors along the trails.
- New attractions can be developed and added to the trail guides.
- Visitors can be led to interesting places which they might otherwise miss.
- Places that become overused and damaged can be removed from the trail for a while.
- The earnings from tourism can be used by the local community.

By working together to improve the services for visitors, the local people are helping to maintain a prosperous economy without damaging the environment or badly upsetting the ways of life which they enjoy.

As yet, there are no major schemes proposed for Aberfeldy by outside developers. However, in many areas there are proposals made for major developments including theme parks, marinas, outdoor activity centres, holiday villages, hotels, etc. They can easily damage the ecology and landscape of an area and upset local people unless carefully planned.

A school group about to go on a guided nature trail.

The area around Aberfeldy has been listed as an Environmentally Sensitive Area. Tourism provides income for local people but the LOCUS group is also ensuring that the environment is protected.

CASE STUDY

Green tourism in Sherwood Forest: a developer's approach

Recreation facilities at Sherwood Forest Village.

New to Britain is the development by the Center Parcs company of holiday villages set in forest areas. These provide a wide range of leisure facilities including villas, a sub-tropical swimming paradise, a sports centre, nature trails and water activities, for people wanting a short break or longer holiday in a countryside environment. The first one was established on 160 hectares of land in Sherwood Forest which had been planted with conifers by the Forestry Commission. Before this site was chosen, the company had worked with the Nature Conservancy Council, the Countryside Commission and the local authority to identify a suitable site.

Before any building took place a thorough ecological survey of the area was carried out so that any special features could be protected or improved. Providing opportunities for guests to experience nature at first hand is one of the features of the village and many new habitats to encourage a greater variety of wildlife have been created. Lakes and streams have been built from scratch, heathland is being developed, 650 000 native broadleaved trees have been planted, open areas have been sown with native grasses and wildflowers, a nature trail and observation hides have been built and a sanctuary for the deer that roam freely over the site has been created. All cars are parked at the entrance, so that people can wander freely and safely in a traffic-free environment.

The purpose of the development is to give people a holiday enjoyable at any time of year.

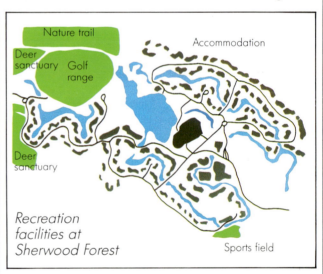

Recreation facilities at Sherwood Forest

Providing a pleasant and varied environment adds to the enjoyment but also benefits the environment. The environment must also be safe for the staying guests. Any pests on plants, for example, are controlled by bringing in other insects that feed on the pest. Protection of the environment has long been a part of the company's policy.

The countryside is used for so many purposes that inevitably there will be conflict between interest groups. Visitors are just one of the groups making demands on the countryside. The challenge is to provide an enjoyable experience without creating problems for the local community or the environment. It would appear that the Sherwood Forest project has been successful in achieving this balance.